Nature's Rooming House

Written by Keith Pigdon
Series Consultant: Linda Hoyt

WorldWise
Content-based Learning

Contents

Introduction

How trees and other plants support life

Just like us, animals and other living things need places to live, where they can gather their food, take shelter, raise their young and protect themselves.

Trees and other large plants are great places for many forms of life to live on, under and near.

Trees are nature's rooming houses. Like rooming houses, trees can provide an environment that supports a **community** of living things. The living things depend on each other for survival. They create communities that we call ecosystems.

Chapter 1

Coastal ecosystems

Wherever the land joins the sea, many animals and plants live together. All these living things create a **community** of life called a coastal ecosystem.

Trees are a vital part of many of these coastal ecosystems. One tree in particular, the mangrove, provides many living things with food, shelter and a place to raise their young.

Examples of coastal ecosystems

Estuary

Mangroves

Salt marsh

Wetlands

The mangrove tree

Mangrove trees grow in coastal wetlands in tropical and subtropical areas.

They thrive in places where freshwater and saltwater meet and have developed a way of dealing with two problems that kill most plants. Plants are very sensitive to salt, and most will die if their root systems are waterlogged and cannot get air.

Mangroves have developed ways of reducing the salt they take in from seawater. Their long roots hold the plant in the mud and filter out most of the salt. The leaves of the mangroves are also able to release salt.

Mangrove trees also send up small roots that can be seen out of the water when the tides are high. They are special "air" roots that are able to breathe air and supply it to the underwater root system. These roots look like **periscopes**.

Find out more

Find out about one of the largest mangrove swamps in the world on the southwest coast of Florida, USA.

Mangrove trees also have a special way of making new plants. The winds blow **pollen** from one tree to another, and after the seeds are formed, they stay attached to the parent tree. They start to grow on the parent tree and when the time is right, they drop into the water and drift away to grow in another place.

This is a little like animals that have live young!

Mangrove swamps support a huge range of life. These swamps receive thc rich **nutrients** from freshwater that runs off the land and is flushed out by the ebb and flow of the tides.

The mudflats may be smelly, boggy places, but they are really important to these ecosystems. Tiny **organisms** called **bacteria** live in the mud and help all other living things by breaking down and **decomposing** dead plants and animals. Their nutrients can then be returned to the ecosystem to support other life.

Life on the roots and around the mangrove shore

Mangrove trees provide food, shelter and places to breed the next generation for a range of animals and plants from tiny to huge.

Hunting birds roost and nest in mangrove swamp **canopy**. They feed extensively on the fish in the mangrove waters.

Hunting birds: Osprey, hawks, southern bald eagles

Lizards live in the trees, feeding on the many kinds of insects that live here.

Lizards: Green anole, brown anole, bark anole

Frogs and toads live on and around the mangrove, feeding on the insect life.

Frogs and toads: Squirrel treefrog, giant toad, **introduced** cuban tree frog

Many mammals can be seen around mangrove swamps.

Mammals: Otters, raccoons, water rats, black bears, skunks, panthers

Nesting birds nest in the mangroves.
Nesting birds: Pelicans, egrets, lesser noddies

Seeds and leaves grow in the canopy. When they fall to the ground, they may be eaten by crabs and birds.

Snakes hunt in the waters and on the trees.
Snakes: Mangrove water snake, rough green tree snake

Wading birds feed in the shallow waters and on the mudflats.
Wading birds: Egrets, spoonbills, herons, sandpipers

Life in the waters

Many plants and animals visit or live around the underwater roots of the mangrove tree.

Plants grow in the shallow waters of the mangroves.

Plants: Algae, seagrasses

Many fish **species** shelter in the mangroves. One-third of all marine species were born and raised in mangrove forests around the world.

Fish: Barramundi, Florida gar

Large reptiles live and feed in the waters and sun themselves on the banks.

Large reptiles: Alligators, crocodiles, turtles

Invertebrates feed around the roots of mangroves.

Invertebrates: Snails, prawns, crabs

Waterbirds dive for fish, plants, crabs and other invertebrates.

Waterbirds: Cormorants, ducks, grebes

Chapter 2

Desert ecosystems

There are many serious challenges for living things in hot deserts. How can they survive with little water? How can they reproduce? How can they protect themselves from the hot sun and cold nights? There are not many large plants in deserts, but they are important to desert ecosystems because they make food, provide homes and shelter, and some even store water.

The saguaro cactus

The saguaro cactus grows in parts of the Sonoran Desert in southwestern United States and northwest Mexico. This cactus is a large treelike plant that stands out in its landscape. Saguaros grow very slowly and some live for more than 150 years. They take ten years to grow about 4 centimetres high. In places with enough rain, they reach 12 to 18 metres. Saguaros develop branches or arms, but it can be 75 years before arms appear.

Saguaro cactuses provide food for animals and water when no other water is available. Birds that live in the desert nest and breed in these plants. There are very few other places to make their nests.

The main stem of the saguaro cactus is thick.

The ribs are covered with long spines that protect the plant from animal attack. These spines point downwards so that water will run onto the cactus or ground below. The skin of the saguaro is covered with a thick waxy coating that keeps the plant dry and prevents it from losing water to the warm desert.

Ribs on the stem contain fleshy tissue that holds water. These ribs expand to store huge amounts of water.

Most of the roots are close to the surface, where the plant can collect any rain that does fall.

Gila woodpecker

Elf owl

Cactus wren

Homes in the cactus

Nest makers

The Gila woodpecker nests in saguaros. It begins by drilling a few small holes before deciding which one to live in. The bird pecks through the skin and between the sharp spines into the soft **tissue**, where the cactus stores water. The cactus fixes the damage by sealing up the inside with **scar tissue** that stops water seeping into the hole and flooding the woodpecker's nest.

Some insects lay their eggs inside the cactus so that their grubs can eat the flesh. The Gila woodpecker can see from the colour of the stem where these grubs are. The bird feeds on the insect **larvae**, and at the same time cuts away the diseased tissue and makes a nest **cavity**. This is a win for the plant and a win for the woodpecker.

The gilded flicker is able to make cavities in the saguaro cactus in much the same way as the Gila woodpecker.

Gilded flicker

Some large hunting birds use the saguaro for nesting and hunting. They construct large nests from sticks between the arms of a large saguaro.

Renting a nest

After the woodpecker or the gilded flicker abandon their cavity, other birds quickly move in. The small American kestrel also uses cavities made or used by other birds as nesting sites. Ravens and great horned owls are known to take over an abandoned hawk nest.

Harris's hawk

House finch

White-winged dove

Feeding on the cactus

Nectar feeders

Saguaros start to produce flowers when they are around 35 years old. The flowers are usually at the end of the main trunk or the arms and sometimes on the side of the plant. Flowers appear from April to June. The **nectar** they produce attracts many animals that feed on it, and move large amounts of **pollen** between the flowers.

The flowers open after sunset and close in mid-afternoon. The flowers last for just one day, but new ones grow each day. At night, the lesser long-nosed bat feeds on the nectar. The main daytime **pollinators** are honeybees and white-winged doves though there are many other animals that enjoy the flowering cactus.

The fruits of the cactus

The flowers of the cactus

Fruit, seed and flesh eaters

After the cactus flower is pollinated, it closes up and dries out as the fruits begin to grow at the base of the flower. As the fruits ripen in June, they are about seven centimetres long and turn a ruby-red colour. Each fruit contains about 2,000 tiny black seeds. These fruits and their seeds provide sweet food for many desert animals that, in turn, spread the seeds throughout the desert.

Many different birds visit the cactus to feed on the fruit. The Gila woodpecker that makes its nest inside the plant takes its fill of the fleshy red pulp growing on its home.

White-winged doves breed during the flowering season of the saguaro cactus. They can feed on the nectar, fruits and seeds of the plant.

Desert mammals also visit the cactus during its fruiting season. Bats that migrated from their winter homes in Mexico to feed on nectar from the flower return to the plant when the fruits ripen. Pack rats, coyotes and other animals join in the feast.

The Sonoran Desert tortoise also eats the fruit.

White-winged dove

Gila woodpecker

Sonoran Desert tortoise

Coyote

Find out more
The fruit of this cactus has been prized by Native Americans for hundreds of years. Find out how the Tohono O'odham people of the Sonoran Desert use the fruit of this plant.

Water storage

In dry times, pack rats, jackrabbits, mule deer and bighorn sheep satisfy their need for water by eating the water-saturated spongy flesh of the cactus.

Jackrabbit

Desert bighorn sheep

Pack rat

Chapter 3

Tropical rainforest ecosystems

Tropical rainforest ecosystems are found in hot, wet places. Rainforests are home to half of all the plant and animal **species** on the earth, but they cover less than 7 per cent of the earth's surface.

Layers of life in a tropical rainforest

Tropical rainforests are made up of different layers.

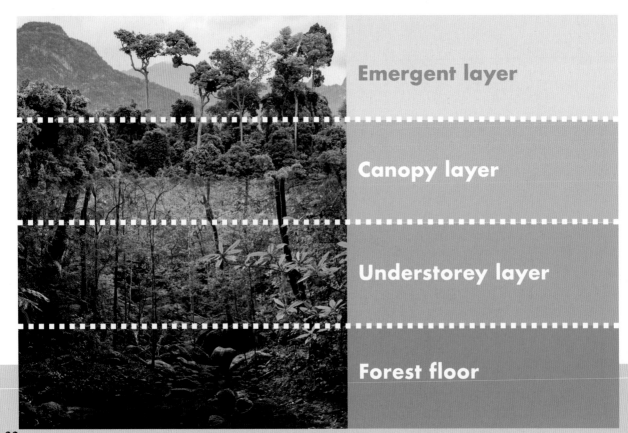

Emergent layer

Canopy layer

Understorey layer

Forest floor

The tallest trees are called the emergent layer. The giant trees in this layer grow to more than 60 metres high, and their trunks can be five metres around. These towering trees take most of the sunlight. They usually have large spreading roots to hold them in the ground.

Trees that grow 18 to 36 metres high above the ground are the **canopy** layer. Their branches may be covered with vines and other plants. These canopy trees are home to most of the living things in the tropical rainforest. They produce millions of smooth oval-shaped leaves that make the sugar and oxygen that living things need for survival.

The middle layer is the understorey layer. Smaller trees that are struggling to reach the canopy grow in this layer. These trees rarely grow higher than 3.5 metres. Their larger leaves catch enough sunlight to make their food.

The forest floor has the soil, rocks, **nutrients** and moisture that the trees and other plants need to grow. Small plants such as grass, ferns, shrubs and wildflowers grow on the forest floor.

Animals in a tropical rainforest

Emergent layer

The towering larger trees of the emergent layer are exposed to fierce tropical sun and the full effects of wind and rain. Life can be difficult for animals here, and most are visitors who come to feed on flowers, fruits and leaves or to nest in hollows.

Harpy eagles make a home base in the tallest rainforest trees. They have the largest **talons** of any eagle, and they use these talons to pluck monkeys, sloths and other prey from the canopy below. Harpy eagles perch in the treetops, waiting for their prey. They often build a large stick nest in the crown of the huge kapok trees.

Other animals that visit this layer include bats, howler and spider monkeys, and butterflies. Scarlet macaws nest in tree hollows, and hummingbirds hover over flowers.

Harpy eagle

Scarlet macaw

Spider monkey

Canopy layer

Canopy layer trees are rich in fruits and seeds and are **teeming** with life. Insects, frogs and other small creatures thrive in the canopy.

Howler monkeys use their long tails to hold onto branches. Their tails allow them to get food that would be out of their reach. Howlers eat leaves, fruit, flowers and birds eggs.

Toucans have adapted to the rainforest canopy by developing long, large bills. This allows them to reach fruit on branches that are too small to support the bird's weight. Toucans build their nests in tree holes and hollows and eat fruit, insects, reptiles and sometimes small animals.

Toucan

Howler monkey

Understorey layer

This layer is dark and hot. Large snakes such as the boa constrictor lie hidden in the branches, waiting for their prey as it passes underneath. Boas wrap their strong bodies around their prey and squeeze their victim until it can no longer breathe. Birds, bats, reptiles, frogs and smaller mammals are their main prey.

Insects such as bees, bullet ants, stick insects, beetles and butterflies live in massive numbers in the understorey. These insects are preyed upon by many kinds of frogs, birds, geckos and other lizards.

Red-eyed tree frogs must live in places where their skin will not dry out. The understorey is perfect. Suction cups on their feet help these frogs to move around in these wet, slippery places.

Jaguars and other large predators spend time hunting in this layer.

Jaguar

Red-eyed tree frog

Boa constrictor

Forest floor

The dark forest floor is where the worms, fungi, **algae** and **bacteria** live. These living things are important because they recycle the nutrients (branches, leaves, fruits, flowers, seeds) that have fallen to the forest floor.

Berry-eating animals such as mice, fruit bats and birds feed in this layer of the forest. Giant anteaters **forage** for ants.

Brightly coloured poison dart frogs live on the forest floor. Their colours warn frog-eating animals that they are dangerous. Scientists believe their poison comes from chemicals in the frog's natural food. Some tropical rainforest plants make their own poisons to protect themselves, and poison dart frogs feed on small insects that eat these poisonous plants.

Giant anteater

Poison dart frog

The web of life in a rainforest

All of these rainforest **organisms** are connected to each other in many different ways. We can understand these connections by thinking about the roles that different organisms play.

Food makers

Food makers get the energy they need by making their own food. Plants are the main food makers on the earth. They are able to use energy from the sun and nutrients in the air and soil to make their own food. So the large trees in forests, small shrubs, the grasses and all the other plants are food makers.

Food eaters

Food eaters cannot make their own food, so they get their energy by feeding on plants or they feed on other animals that eat plants.

There are three types of food eaters:

- Plant eaters – Herbivores
- Plant and meat eaters – Omnivores
- Meat eaters – Carnivores

Recyclers

Recyclers feed on decaying plants and animals. Their feeding activity allows them to survive, and at the same time it returns nutrients from the decaying plants and animals to the soil. This helps the plants get the nutrients that they need to grow. Worms, fungi and bacteria are nature's recyclers that break down things that were once living.

Food makers

Herbivore

Omnivore

Carnivore

Nutrients

Recyclers

Conclusion

When we visit areas where there are magnificent trees, we appreciate their beauty, the shade they offer, and the birds and larger animals we can see on and around them.

However, there is so much more in nature's rooming houses that we may not see or understand. All the living and non-living things that live on and around trees are important parts of that ecosystem. In a way, they help each other to survive.

Glossary

algae plant-like living things that can make their own food, mostly found in water

bacteria tiny living things that have only one cell

canopy the highest layer of branches in a tree or group of trees

cavity a hole or hollow space

community a group of plants and animals living together in the same place

decomposing breaking down slowly into smaller and smaller parts

forage to search for food

introduced plants or animals that have been brought to a place for the first time, and start living there

invertebrates a group of animals that do not have backbones

larvae the young form of many insects that hatch from eggs and turn into a very different form as an adult

nectar a sweet, sugary liquid that is made by plants

nutrients the parts in food that living things need to survive and grow

organisms individual living things

periscopes tube-like instruments with mirrors that are used to look above the surface of the water, especially from inside a submarine

pollen tiny, dust-like particles found in plants that are needed to produce seeds

pollinators animals like bees that transfer pollen from one flower to another

scar tissue the groups of cells that form after damage is done to a part of a plant or animal

species a group of living things that are alike in many ways, have many traits in common and are able to have offspring

talons sharp claws that are found on the feet of some birds

teeming to be full or overflowing with something

tissue groups of cells that form parts of a plant or animal

Index